Date: 12/5/16

J 615.7922 ORR
Orr, Tamra,
Antibiotics /

Antibiotics

TAMRA B. ORR

Children's Press®
An Imprint of Scholastic Inc.

Content Consultant

Phyllis Meadows, PhD, MSN, RN

Associate Dean for Practice, Clinical Professor, Health Management and Policy

University of Michigan, Ann Arbor, Michigan

Library of Congress Cataloging-in-Publication Data

Names: Orr, Tamra, author.

Title: Antibiotics / Tamra B. Orr.

Other titles: True book.

Description: New York, NY : Children's Press, an imprint of Scholastic Inc., [2016] | Series: A true book | Includes bibliographical references and index.

Identifiers: LCCN 2016013908| ISBN 9780531218600 (library binding) | ISBN 9780531227787 (pbk.)

Subjects: LCSH: Antibiotics—Juvenile literature. | Medicine—History—Juvenile literature. | Bacteria—Effect of drugs on—Juvenile literature.

Classification: LCC RM267 .O77 2016 | DDC 615.7/922—dc23

LC record available at https://lccn.loc.gov/2016013908

© 2017 Scholastic Inc.

All rights reserved. Published in 2017 by Children's Press, an imprint of Scholastic Inc.

Printed in China 62

SCHOLASTIC, CHILDREN'S PRESS, A TRUE BOOK™, and associated logos are trademarks and/or registered trademarks of Scholastic Inc.

1 2 3 4 5 6 7 8 9 10 R 26 25 24 23 22 21 20 19 18 17

Front cover: A medical researcher in protective clothing

Back cover: Insects in test tubes being studied as possible sources of new antibiotics

Find the Truth!

Everything you are about to read is true *except* for one of the sentences on this page.

Which one is **TRUE**?

T or F Antibiotics are not as effective today as they were in the past.

T or F Antibiotics are used to treat viruses.

Find the answers in this book.

Contents

1 A World Full of Germs

What are antibiotics? **7**

2 The First Steps

What were some of the earliest
antibacterial discoveries? **15**

THE **BIG** TRUTH!

A Natural Cure

What ingredients are scientists using to
create the latest antibiotics?. **22**

Lavender

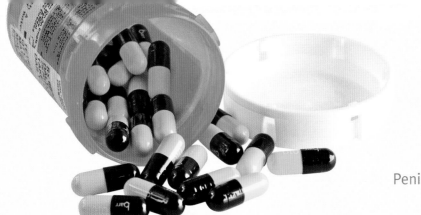

Penicillin

3 Fleming's Mold Juice

How did Alexander Fleming discover modern
antibiotics? **25**

4 A Pressing Public Health Problem

How are bacteria changing and what
can we do to fight them? **33**

True Statistics **44**

Resources **45**

Important Words **46**

Index **47**

About the Author **48**

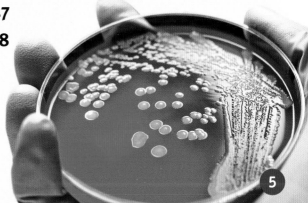

MRSA bacteria

After getting a cut or scrape, it is a good idea to wash the wound to kill germs.

CHAPTER 1

A World Full of Germs

The world is full of germs. They are too tiny to see without a microscope, but these **microorganisms** are everywhere. They have many ways of getting into your body. You can breathe them in through your nose or mouth. You can also touch a germ-covered object and then touch your nose, eyes, or mouth. Germs can even get into your body through cuts or scrapes.

More germs are exchanged shaking hands than kissing.

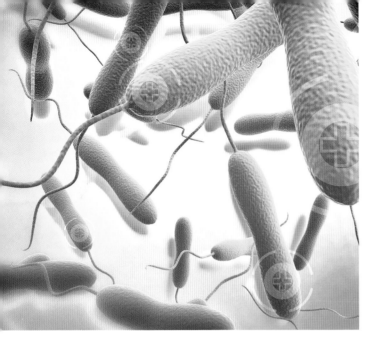

Bacteria are so small that they can't be seen without a microscope.

The average adult human body contains 2 to 6 pounds (0.9 to 2.7 kilograms) of bacteria.

The Germ Theory

Bacteria are among the most common kinds of germs. Once they are inside your body, these microorganisms multiply and grow. Some bacteria can cause serious illnesses or just make you feel a little sick. The idea that illnesses are caused by microorganisms is called the germ theory. The germ theory was first suggested in the mid-16th century. However, it took centuries to become widely accepted.

What Are Antibiotics?

Antibiotics are substances that fight against bacteria. It may surprise you to learn that the word *antibiotic* means "against life." Because antibiotics have saved countless lives, this seems like the wrong name. However, it actually describes antibiotics very well. Bacteria are alive, and they can be killed by antibiotics.

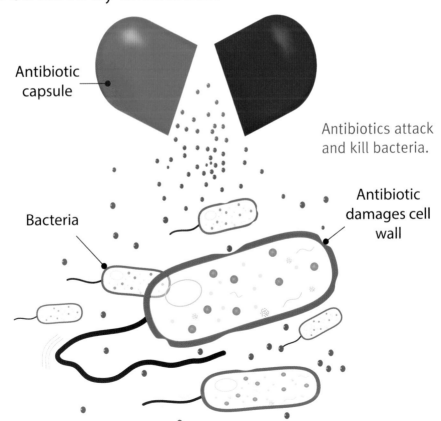

Antibiotic capsule

Antibiotics attack and kill bacteria.

Bacteria

Antibiotic damages cell wall

Honey, Bread, and Beer

Imagine that you fall and cut your knee while you are playing outside. A few days later, your knee really hurts. It is red and swollen. If you lived in ancient Egypt, your mother might cover your knee in honey or give you a glass of beer. In ancient China or Greece, she might press a piece of moldy bread on the wound. In Russia, she might have used warm dirt.

Honey has antibiotic properties.

Even though these ancient cultures did not know about bacteria, their treatments acted as antibiotics. Honey contains **hydrogen peroxide**. This kills bacteria. Beer is made from **fermented** grains. It was full of tetracycline, a type of antibiotic still used today. Bread mold is also a type of antibiotic, and there can be bacteria-killing substances in dirt.

Millions of bacteria live in dirt. They help keep the plants growing there healthy.

There are more bacteria in your mouth than there are people in the world.

11

How Do Antibiotics Work?

Antibiotics can be pills, injections, or a cream you rub into your skin. After you take the medicine, antibiotics either kill the bacteria in your body or keep them from multiplying. As the bacteria in your body are weakened, you start to feel better. There are often side effects to antibiotics, though. Some people have **digestive** problems and feel sick to their stomach when they use antibiotics. Others get diarrhea.

Antibiotics cannot tell the difference between "good" and "bad" bacteria.

A Different Kind of Sickness

Antibiotics are not able to treat every condition. Some sicknesses are caused by microorganisms called **viruses** instead of bacteria. These cannot be treated with antibiotics. Viruses and bacteria are often confused. Both are types of germs. However, viruses are much smaller than bacteria. They can reproduce only by attaching themselves to **cells**. Viruses cause such illnesses as colds, the flu, and **bronchitis**.

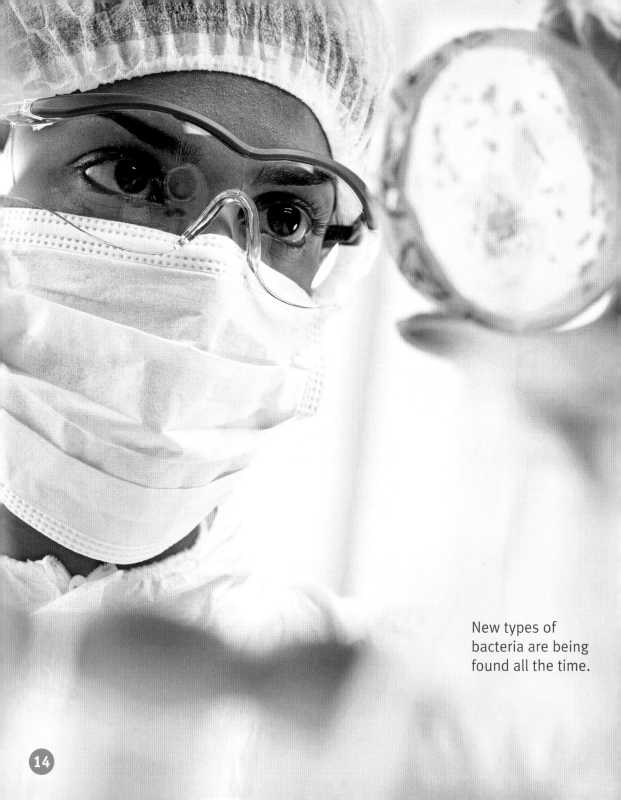

New types of
bacteria are being
found all the time.

The First Steps

Before the link between bacteria and illness was discovered, doctors did not understand the cause of many common sicknesses. But by the late 1800s, the germ theory was being accepted by the scientific world. Once people learned that bacteria could make people sick, the next step was to find a way to fight bacterial infections.

Researchers have found 1,458 new species of bacteria just in belly buttons.

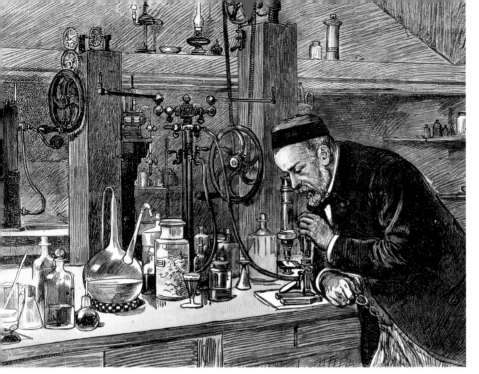

Scientists have been studying bacteria and other germs for more than 100 years.

A Long Process

Scientists began searching for treatments that could stop bacteria from multiplying or that could even kill bacteria entirely. This was not a simple process, however. As with most of history's most important inventions, modern antibiotics came as a result of the work of many people. These innovators worked for decades to solve the mystery of bacteria one clue at a time.

Chemicals and Cleanliness

One of the first medical professionals to find ways of fighting bacteria was an English surgeon named Joseph Lister. In the 1860s, he was desperate to lower the number of patients whose wounds were infected during surgery. Many times, an operation would go well, but the patient would die of an infection days later. What could be done to fight these infections?

Joseph Lister realized the importance of keeping germs away from wounds.

Lister began soaking patients' bandages in **carbolic acid** after reading that it killed germs. He also did something most people take for granted today: He washed his hands and surgical instruments before each operation.

Lister's methods were successful. Infections dropped dramatically. Other doctors began using his methods in their operating rooms. Lister became known as the "father of **antiseptic** surgery."

The rate of infections among patients dropped when doctors began to adopt Lister's practices.

Two Curious Germans

In the 1880s, German doctors Rudolf Emmerich and Oscar Loew had an idea. They wondered if the germs that caused one sickness could cure another one. To find out, they used the bandages of infected patients to grow germs in test tubes. Next, they put these bacteria into test tubes full of the germs that caused four other diseases. The plan was a success. The first bacteria destroyed the rest.

Rudolf Emmerich (pictured) partnered with Oscar Loew to experiment with early antibiotic techniques.

Emmerich and Loew used the results of this experiment to create a new medication. It was the first official antibiotic. By 1899, the medicine was being used in hospitals. Although it helped many people, it also proved **toxic** in some cases. A number of patients died, and doctors stopped using the treatment. They needed a better medicine—and soon.

During the 19th century, patients were often kept in close quarters in hospitals.

Moldy bread may look gross, but it can be used to kill harmful bacteria.

It would be a few more decades until the first major breakthrough in antibiotics. When it finally happened, it was based on a treatment that had existed for centuries. Do you remember how ancient people sometimes used moldy bread to treat wounds? This same idea led to the biggest discovery in the history of antibiotics.

A Natural Cure

The majority of antibiotics used in the United States are given to livestock such as chickens and cows. Over time, these animals have developed a resistance to the medications. This means the medication is less effective. Humans are experiencing similar problems with antibiotics.

Nature just might have the solution many health-care professionals are looking for. After all, many other medications are made from natural substances. For example, aspirin is made from willow bark. Cough and cold medications are often made from mint plants.

Mint

Some farmers are trying natural antibiotics such as oregano and cinnamon oils instead of standard antibiotic medications. So far, these products have been helpful.

Cinnamon

Studies have found a lot of promise in using lavender and other natural ingredients in new medications for humans. These new ingredients may help patients who have become resistant to standard antibiotics.

Lavender

An eye doctor
in ancient Egypt
performs a treatment
on a patient.

CHAPTER 3

Fleming's Mold Juice

Ancient people thought mold had magic powers that could drive away the evil spirits they believed caused sickness. They were half right. Mold isn't magic, but some kinds do have antibacterial properties. The man who made this discovery, Alexander Fleming, figured out by accident how to create antibiotics from mold. As he once said, "One sometimes finds what one is not looking for."

Ancient Egyptian eyeliner may have helped protect the eyes from disease.

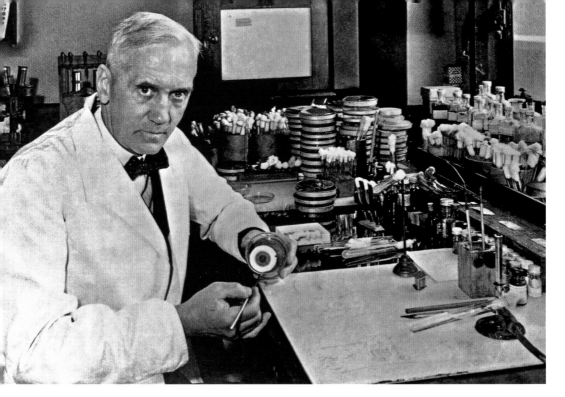

Alexander Fleming poses in his laboratory.

A Clue in the Clutter

Alexander Fleming was a British scientist who had seen firsthand how dangerous bacteria were to wounded soldiers. He had been on the front lines of World War I. He knew that infection was a bigger threat than any of the enemy's weapons. He was determined to find a way to stop bacterial infections and save lives.

In 1928 and 1929, Fleming had been experimenting with different types of bacteria. His lab was a mess. It was covered in petri dishes. Each one held colorful batches of bacteria from previous experiments. As he was cleaning, Fleming noticed something. One of the dishes looked different. A bit of mold had gotten into it. Fleming looked closer. All around the mold, the bacteria had disappeared.

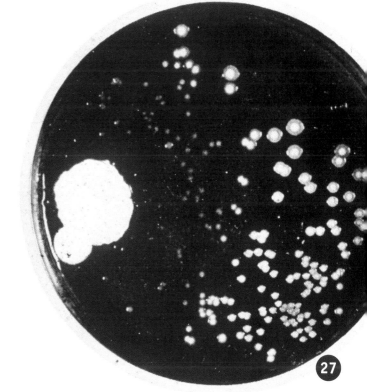

This photograph shows the actual dish of mold from Fleming's discovery.

Fleming grabbed his camera and took a picture of the mold. He took a sample of what he called "the fluff in the dish" and created a mixture from it. Other lab workers teased Fleming about his "mold juice." Because the mold he had used was named *Penicillium notatum*, Fleming called his creation penicillin. Now it was time to put this new antibiotic to the test.

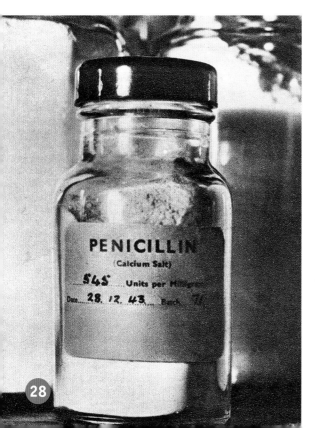

For his discovery of penicillin, Fleming was awarded the Nobel Prize in Physiology or Medicine in 1945.

PENICILLIN
(Calcium Salt)
545 Units per Milligram
Date 28. 12. 43. Batch 76

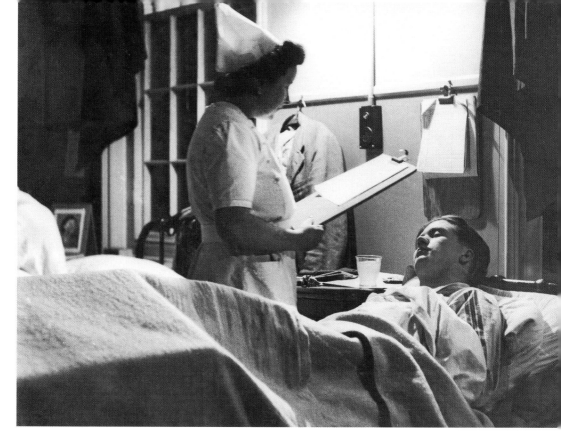

A nurse checks on a patient during World War II.

Fleming gave penicillin to sick lab mice. He was thrilled when the medication made the mice healthy again. However, the journey from curing lab mice to treating sick people was long. It took several years of hard work by Fleming and other scientists before penicillin could be used routinely—just in time to help soldiers wounded in World War II.

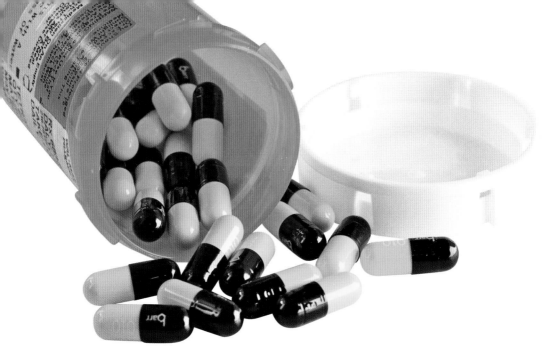

Penicillin is just one of many antibiotic medications available today.

The Golden Era

Fleming's work inspired many scientists to develop other types of antibiotics. As much of a "wonder drug" as penicillin was, it could not treat all bacterial illnesses successfully. A wider variety of antibiotics was needed. Between the 1950s and 1970s, many new bacteria-fighting medications were developed. It was a golden era for medical research.

Since the 1970s, very few new antibiotics have been discovered. Instead, most scientists have focused on improving the medications we already have. Making antibiotics more effective is very important, however. Just as scientists are constantly working to improve medications, bacteria are always growing stronger and finding ways to resist antibiotics.

We still have a lot to learn about bacteria and antibiotics.

Cockroaches and locusts might be sources for future antibiotics.

CHAPTER 4

A Pressing Public Health Problem

People have relied on antibiotics for many years. These medications were very effective and some people ended up taking them too often. Some started getting prescriptions for antibiotics at a very early age and kept taking the medicine at many times in their lives. Others took the medicine for viral infections, even though antibiotics cannot treat these illnesses. Some were overly exposed to antibiotics through medications such as certain acne treatments.

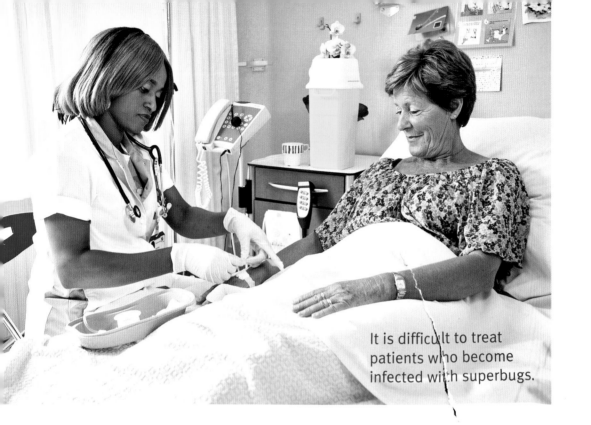

It is difficult to treat patients who become infected with superbugs.

A Growing Resistance

Each time antibiotics are taken, most of the bacteria causing the illness are killed. Some survive, though. Over time, these extra-tough bacteria can change into "superbugs." These superbugs are creating an international health problem known as antibiotic resistance. This is when antibiotics that once killed the bacteria no longer work.

One of the most challenging superbugs to fight is called methicillin-resistant *Staphylococcus aureus* (MRSA). This bacteria first appeared in 1960. It is resistant to antiseptics. This means that even when an area is cleaned thoroughly, MRSA bacteria might remain. MRSA is especially common in hospitals, and patients often get infected during surgery. However, a growing number of MRSA cases are developing outside hospitals as a result of everyday injuries such as paper cuts and skinned knees.

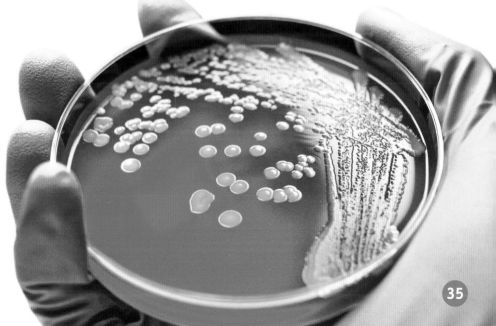

A researcher holds a dish of MRSA bacteria that have formed on a blood sample.

Antibiotic resistance is a serious problem. It has been called a "ticking time bomb" and one of the "biggest threats to global health today." Experts believe that by 2050, as many as 10 million people around the world will die from some type of superbug. In response, governments and other organizations are devoting millions of dollars to new antibiotics research.

Drug companies are constantly creating new medications to fight newly discovered illnesses.

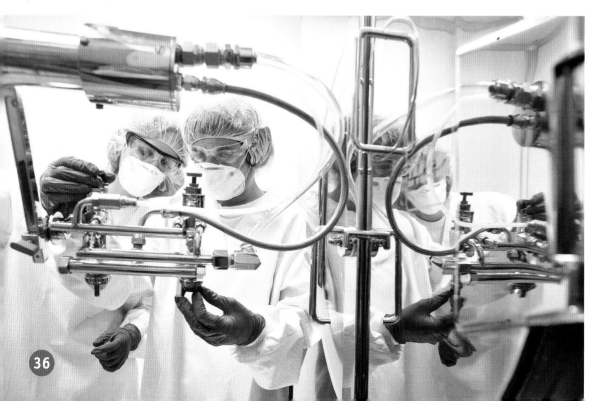

Only around 70 percent of people wash their hands after using the toilet.

Germ Manners

It is impossible to avoid all germs, but you can help stop them from spreading. At any time, there are between 10,000 and 10 million bacteria on each of your hands. After using the toilet, the number of germs on your fingertips doubles. This means you should always wash your hands after using the bathroom. Use warm water and soap, and dry your hands well when you are done.

It is always important to follow a doctor's instructions closely when taking medications.

Following the Rules

There are important rules to follow when taking antibiotics. A certain level of medication is needed to destroy the bacteria in your body. You must always take the full amount prescribed by your doctor. Even if you feel better, you have to keep taking the antibiotic until it is gone. Otherwise, your illness might return. When it comes back, the bacteria might be more resistant to antibiotics. ★

The Proper Prescription

While improper use of antibiotics can lead to antibiotic-resistant bacteria, this class of medicine remains an important weapon against certain illnesses. Your doctor might give you antibiotics to fight off sicknesses such as Lyme disease, pneumonia, strep throat, or bronchitis. You might also take antibiotics to help with an ear or sinus infection, or if bacteria infect a cut, scrape, or other wound. Taken correctly, antibiotics will have you feeling better in no time!

Many common types of ear infections are caused by bacteria.

43

True Statistics

Number of antibiotic prescriptions written in the United States each year: 262.5 million

Number of people infected with antibiotic-resistant bacteria in the United States each year: At least 2 million

Number of people who die from antibiotic-resistant bacteria in the United States each year: At least 23,000

Percentage of U.S. antibiotic prescriptions considered unnecessary by the CDC: Around 50 percent

Number of U.S. patients who acquire bacterial infections from hospitals each year: Nearly 2 million

Year the last new antibiotic was discovered: 2016

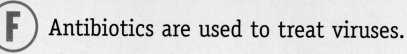
Did you find the truth?

T Antibiotics are not as effective today as they were in the past.

F Antibiotics are used to treat viruses.

Resources

Books

Barnard, Bryn. *Outbreak: Plagues That Changed History*. New York: Dragonfly Books, 2015.

Burillo-Kirch, Christine. *Microbes: Discover an Unseen World*. White River Junction, VT: Nomad Press, 2015.

Goldsmith, Connie. *Superbugs Strike Back: When Antibiotics Fail*. Minneapolis, MN: Twenty-First Century Books, 2006.

Rooney, Anne. *You Wouldn't Want to Live Without Antibiotics!* New York: Children's Press, 2014.

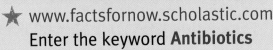

Visit this Scholastic Web site for more information on antibiotics:

★ www.factsfornow.scholastic.com
Enter the keyword **Antibiotics**

Important Words

antiseptic (an-ti-SEP-tik) a substance that kills germs and prevents infection by stopping the growth of germs

bacteria (bak-TEER-ee-uh) microscopic, single-celled living things that exist everywhere and can be either helpful or harmful

bronchitis (brahng-KYE-tis) a disease of the bronchial tubes inside the lungs

carbolic acid (kar-BAH-lik AS-id) a chemical that can be used to kill germs

cells (SELZ) the smallest units of an animal or plant

digestive (dye-JES-tiv) having to do with the process of breaking down food and separating from it the things that the body needs

fermented (fur-MEN-tid) turned into alcohol

hydrogen peroxide (HYE-druh-juhn puh-RAHK-side) a chemical that can be used to kill germs

microorganisms (mye-kroh-OR-guh-niz-uhmz) living things that are so small that they can be seen only with a microscope

toxic (TAHK-sik) poisonous

viruses (VYE-ruhs-iz) very tiny organisms that can reproduce and grow only when inside living cells

Index

Page numbers in **bold** indicate illustrations.

ancient cultures, 10–11, 21, **24**, 25
antibiotic resistance, 22–23, 31, 34, 35, 36, 42

bacteria, **8**, **9**, 12, 27, 31, 34, **35**, 38, 41
bacteriophage, **37**
beer, 10, 11

carbolic acid, 18

diarrhea, 12
dirt, 10, 11, 38
doctors, 15, 18, 20, **24**, **42**

ear infections, **43**
Emmerich, Rudolf, **19**–20

Fleming, Alexander, 25, **26**–29, 38

germs, 7, 8, 13, 41
germ theory, 8, 15

honey, **10**, 11
hospitals, **20**, 35, **38**
hydrogen peroxide, **11**

illnesses, 8, **13**, 15, 19, 30, 33, **36**, **40**, 42, **43**
injuries, **6**, 7, 35, 43
instructions, **42**

Lister, Joseph, **17**–**18**, **38**
Loew, Oscar, 19–20

methicillin-resistant *Staphylococcus aureus* (MRSA) **35**, 38, **39**
mold, 10, 11, **21**, 25, **27**–28

nanobots, **40**
natural antibiotics, **23**
Nobel Prize, 28

overuse, **32**, 33, 34

penicillin, **28**–**29**, **30**, **38**
phage therapy, **37**
prevention, **41**

research, **16**, **18**, 19–20, 23, **26**–29, 30–**31**, **35**, **36**, 38
resistance. *See* antibiotic resistance.

side effects, **12**
superbugs, **34**, 35, 36, 37, 38–39
surgery, 17–**18**, 35
synthetic antibiotics, 39

teixobactin, 38
tetracycline, 11
timeline, **38**–**39**

viruses, 13, **37**

washing, **6**, 18, **41**
word meaning, 9
World War I, 26
World War II, **29**

About the Author

Tamra Orr is the author of hundreds of books for readers of all ages. She has a degree in English and Secondary Education from Ball State University, and now lives in the Pacific Northwest. She is the mother of four children, and loves to spend her free time reading, writing, and going camping. She tries to stay healthy, but is always grateful for antibiotics for those times she isn't!